Newport Mansions

Postcards from the Gilded Age

Residence of Louis Bruguiere, Newport, R. I.

Villa of Dr. H. Barton Jacobs, Newport, R. I.

Tunnel on Cliff Walk, Newport, R.I.

Federico Santi
and John Gacher

Schiffer® Publishing Ltd

4880 Lower Valley Road, Atglen, PA 19310 USA

If you wish to contact the authors, they may be reached at The Drawing Room Antiques, located at 152 Spring Street, Newport, RI 02840 USA or by phone at 401-841-5060. Online they may be reached at <www.drawrm.com>.

Other Schiffer Books by Federico Santi and John Gacher
Art Nouveau Ironwork of Austria & Hungary
Zsolnay Ceramics: Collecting a Culture

Other Schiffer Books on Related Subjects
Cape Cod Memories: An Illustrated History in Postcards, by Mary L. Martin and Karen Choppa
Greetings from Havre de Grace, by David Craig and Mary L. Martin
Greetings from New Orleans: A History in Postcards, by Mary L. Martin and Tina Skinner
Greetings from Ohio: Vintage Postcards 1900-1960s, by Robert Reed
Greetings from Savannah, by Mary L. Martin, Tina Skinner, and Nathaniel Wolfgang-Price
Newport News: A Vintage Postcard Tour, by Harold Cones and John Bryant
Santa Fe & Taos: A History in Postcards, by Mary L. Martin and Ginny Parfitt

Library of Congress Control Number: 2006924184

Designed by Mark David Bowyer
Type set in Shelley Allegro BT / Aldine 721 BT

ISBN: 0-7643-2497-7
Printed in China

Published by Schiffer Publishing Ltd.
4880 Lower Valley Road
Atglen, PA 19310
Phone: (610) 593-1777; Fax: (610) 593-2002
E-mail: Info@schifferbooks.com

For the largest selection of fine reference books on this and related subjects, please visit our web site at **www.schifferbooks.com**
We are always looking for people to write books on new and related subjects. If you have an idea for a book please contact us at the above address.

This book may be purchased from the publisher.
Include $3.95 for shipping.
Please try your bookstore first.
You may write for a free catalog.

In Europe, Schiffer books are distributed by
Bushwood Books
6 Marksbury Ave.
Kew Gardens
Surrey TW9 4JF England
Phone: 44 (0) 20 8392-8585; Fax: 44 (0) 20 8392-9876
E-mail: info@bushwoodbooks.co.uk
Website: www.bushwoodbooks.co.uk
Free postage in the U.K., Europe; air mail at cost.

Contents

Acknowledgments

Whether they realized it or not, many people have helped and encouraged the production of this book. Mrs. Peter (Gladys) Bolhouse started our interest in collecting Newport postcards many years ago. She was the Curator of Manuscripts at the Newport Historical Society and though she is no longer with us, her spirit lives on in that marvelous institution. Paul Miller of the Newport Preservation Society has always been there to answer questions about Newport architecture and life in the Gilded Age. Bert Lippincott, Librarian of the Newport Historical Society, was invaluable in helping with Society archives. Paul Szapary and Diana Sylvaria gave editorial support and encouragement and shared historical information at crucial times.

Introduction

"Our moments of destiny steal upon us so quietly, generally so unperceived, that we are hardly aware of them until they have passed by. Only in after years can we look back on them and see them for their true perspective, know that they made or marred our whole lives."

—Elizabeth Drexel Lehr, *King Lehr and The Gilded Age*

Newport, Rhode Island has been a tourist destination since the mid nineteenth century. Numerous guides, tourist brochures, maps, and articles over the past 150 years have celebrated the charms of this "City by the Sea." By the end of the nineteenth century, America's nouveau riche society had declared that Newport was the place to be and the place to be seen—at least in the summertime. Soon the construction boom of what were to be known as Newport "cottages" led to a veritable avalanche of opulence ushering in the Gilded Age. Bellevue Avenue and the land surrounding Ocean Drive in Newport became home to palatial mansions, one more spectacular than the next, all to be used for no more than three months in the summer. Most were in open view of the street, easily seen by the public and the owners' society rivals.

Thousands of tourists flocked to Newport to see how the new "American royalty" lived. For most, the typical memento of their visit was a postcard—the Gilded Age mansions of Newport were memorialized on 3.5" x 5" pieces of cardboard. Most of the great homes were pictured this way and cards were mailed all over the world, spreading the word that Newport truly was "The Queen of Resorts."

Collecting Newport postcards today is not difficult. Thousands were published through the decades and most have found their way into collections and dealers' inventories. Most of the important mansions were pictured throughout the years, hence as many as thirty different views for mansions such as The Breakers or Marble House may be available. In this book, we present postcards showing the more popular Gilded Age mansions, beach views, and scenes of Bellevue Avenue shopping and entertainment sites.

Today, the Gilded Age is alive and well in Newport, as recreated by the Preservation Society of Newport County and The Newport Restoration Foundation. Tourists arrive by the thousands each year to visit the insides of these architectural wonders—and to learn about life in the Gilded Age during the late nineteenth and early twentieth centuries.

The following online web sites will be of help when planning a visit to Newport:

The Preservation Society of Newport County
(www.newportmansions.org)

The Newport Restoration Foundations
(www.newportrestoration.com)

The Newport Historical Society
(www.newporthistorical.org)

The Newport Mansions Review
(www.newportmansionsreview.com)

A word about the postcard captions:

For each postcard in this book, the printed information from the picture side of the card will be listed first in italics, followed by the approximate date of the card (often a postmark date), any written messages by the sender, and (if indicated) the authors' commentary.

Value Guide to Newport Postcards

In today's marketplace, Newport postcards showing images of mansions, beaches, and city views generally sell for between $4.00 and $8.00. Photo postcards, which were produced in smaller numbers and are therefore less available, generally sell in the $6.00 to $15.00 price range.

There are exceptions to these guidelines, however. If a collector "needs" a particular card, usually he or she is willing to pay more. In addition, some cards had smaller production runs and were simply more rare; these can command prices of over $20.00 for one card. Condition, of course, is always a factor in value: marred and bent cards should sell for less.

There is no doubt that ephemera values have been increasing over the years. Cards that we saw on the marketplace selling for a dollar or less twenty years ago are now frequently offered for $4.00 or $5.00.

Collectors can start out buying cards by category: mansions, street scenes, the Navy, etc. We prefer used cards with personal messages written on the front or back. These notes offer a glimpse into the times in which the card was mailed and do not detract from the value. Collecting Newport postcards is a great hobby, and with the thousands of cards printed over the last hundred years, it is easy to assemble a wonderful collection.

Chapter One

Newport Cliff Walk

Tourists have been visiting Newport's Cliff Walk since the mid-nineteenth century. Starting at the top of Easton's Beach (also called Newport Beach and First Beach), the pedestrian walkway winds along the coast and cliffs all the way to Bailey's Beach. The Walk is three and a half miles long and was designated a National Recreation Trail several years ago. On one side are views of the Atlantic Ocean with Middletown in the distance, on the other side are views of the cottages built by the rich and famous summer colonists.

Postcards of the Cliff Walk and the mansions along the way have been produced since the turn of the twentieth century and continue to be produced today. We estimate that over a thousand different cards of the Cliff Walk have been printed in the last one hundred years. This chapter presents a sampling of those cards, showing the view as you walk from Easton's Beach toward Bailey's Beach.

Tens of thousands of tourists visit the Cliff Walk each year and much time and effort has been expended into making it a safe and pleasurable walking experience. The Walk is open dawn to dusk without charge. For further information about the Cliff Walk, go online to <www.cliffwalk.com>.

PLANS, MAPS AND FULL PARTICULARS AT
NEW YORK OFFICE

1905

Newport Villas

FOR RENT FOR THE SEASON OF 1905

—BY—

DEBLOIS & ELDRIDGE

NEWPORT AND
NEW YORK
REAL ESTATE

152 BELLEVUE AVENUE, NEWPORT, R. I.

TELEPHONE, NEWPORT OFFICE, No. 324

5 EAST 33d STREET, NEW YORK

TELEPHONE, NEW YORK, OFFICE; 3323 MADISON SQUARE

Newport real estate was in such demand that villas could be rented for the season for up to $12,000.00—and that was for three months only (see following page).

FULL PARTICULARS OF ANY OF THE FOLLOWING HOUSES CAN BE OBTAINED AT NO. 5 EAST 33rd STREET WHERE MAPS AND PLANS CAN BE SEEN.

HOUSES FROM $3,100 TO $12,000.

	Baldwin Estate (s)	Bellevue Avenue
	Bearhaven Realty Co. (s))sea view)	Beacon Hill
	Bennett, J. G. (s) "Stone Villa"	Bellevue Avenue
	Chanler, Winthrop (sea view)	Cliffs
	Coats, A. M. (s) (sea view)	Brenton Road
	Cramp, Mrs. E. S. (s)	Bellevue Avenue
	Duryea, Mrs. H. B. (s) (harbor view)	Beacon Hill Road
	Eldridge, Mrs· J. H. (s) (sea view)	Ochre Point
	Gibert Estate (s)	Bellevue Avenue
RENTED.	Havemeyer Estate (s)	Bellevue Avenue
	Hodgson Estate (s)	Bellevue Avenue
	Marquand Estate (s)	Rhode Island Avenue
	McKay Estate (s)	Marine Avenue
RENTED.	Morrell, E. V. (s)	Shepard Avenue
	Osgood Estate (s)	Bellevue Avenue
	Pendleton Estate, (s)	The Cliffs
	Pratt, Mrs H. R.	Bellevue Avenue
	Reed Mrs. J. Van D. (s) (sea view)	Bellevue Avenue
	Shields Estate (s) (sea view)	Ruggles Avenue
RENTED.	Tiffany, Mrs. George (s)	Narragansett Avenue
RENTED.	Train Place, (s) (sea view)	Bellevue Avenue
RENTED.	Warren Estate (s)	Narragansett Avenue
	White, Mrs. Henry (s) (harbor view)	Harrison Avenue

HOUSES FROM $1,600 TO $3,000.

	Barret, Mrs. E. E. (s)	Catherine Street
	Best, Mrs. C. L. (s)	Bellevue Avenue
RENTED.	Bruen Estate, (s) "The Villino,"	Bellevue Avenue
	Cadwalader, John (s)	Bellevue Avenue
	Cleveland, Dr. Clement (s)	Catherine Street
	Cushman, E. C. (s)	Catherine Street
	Foster, Mrs. Frank (s)	Catherine Street
	Garrettson, F. P. (s)	Mill Street
	Gilliatt, C. G. (s) (2)	Rhode Island Avenue
	Hartshorn Estate (s) (harbor view)	Halidon Hill
	Hone, Miss A. R. (s)	Greenough Place
	Mason, Miss (s) ("Brent Lodge")	Gibbs Avenue
	Pinard Cottages,	Narragansett Avenue
	Pumpelly, Raphael (s) (sea view)	Gibbs Avenue
	Satterlee Estate, (s)	Clay Street
	Smith, J. Clinch (s) (sea view)	Harrison Avenue
	Stockton, Mrs. P. A. (s)	Bellevue Avenue
	Swan, J. A. (s) (sea view) (Cooke Cottage)	Gibbs Avenue
	Walter, Mrs. Howard	Oakwood Terrace
	Weaver, Benj (s)	Ayrault Street
	Whipple Estate (sea view)	Sea View Avenue
	Whitwell Estate (s)	Berkeley Avenue
	Woolsey, Miss	Rhode Island Avenue

(s) signifies stable.

HOUSES FROM $500 TO $1,500.

	Armistead, Mrs. W. K, (sea view)	Hunter Avenue
	Arnold Estate (s)	Rhode Island Avenue
RENTED.	Austin, Amory,	Ayrault Street
	Buffum, W. P. (s)	Greenough Place
	Bull Cottages, (s) (2)	One Mile Corner
	Case, P. H. (s)	Kay Street
	Cliff Cottages, (sea view)	Cliff Avenue
RENTED.	Collins Estate, (s)	Cottage Street
	Cortazzo, Mrs. E. C. (sea view)	Sea View Avenue
	DeBlois Cottage, (sea view)	Gibbs Avenue
RENTED.	Dresser Cottage,	Bellevue Court
	Engs Cottage,	Kay Street
	Eustis Cottages,	Eustis Avenue
	Hall Cottages, (s)	Easton's Beach
	Hartshorn, Mrs. E. H. G. (harbor view)	Halidon Hill
	Henshaw, J. H.	Beach View Avenue
	Herrick, E. J. (s)	Clay Street
RENTED.	Hodgson Estate, "Willowbank" (s)	Spring Street
RENTED.	Howland, Mrs. Joseph	Rhode Island Avenue
	Janney, Thomas	Narragansett Avenue
	King Estate, (s)	Ayrault street

(s) signifies stable.

WE HAVE HOUSES WHICH THE OWNERS DESIRE NOT TO HAVE LISTED BUT WHICH COULD BE RENTED.

DWELLINGS FOR SALE. **FOR SALE. BUILDING SITES IN ALL PARTS OF THE CITY.**

Newport, RI Bathing Beach. c. 1906. A view of Easton's Beach with the Cliff Walk shown in the upper left of the image.

Newport R.I. Entrance to Cliff Walk showing Beach. c. 1906. The road by the electric lines was then called Bath Road; today it is called Memorial Boulevard.

Newport Beach from the Cliff Walk, Newport, R.I. On the back of the card is printed: *Is considered one of the finest beaches on the Atlantic Coast, and is one of the many beautiful summer attractions of Newport. Is unique on account of its Bath Houses.* c. 1923. The hand written message states: "Are Staying at BelleVue House. Will be home Monday night. Auntie May."

New Cliff Hotel, Newport, R.I. c. 1906. The Newport Casino Bulletin of 1904 lists an ad for the New Cliffs Hotel, in which it states: "Charmingly situated on the famous Cliff Walk, Newport's only hotel on the water and convenient to the Bathing Beach. The hotel contains many attractive rooms, single or en suite, with porcelain baths and strictly up-to-date plumbing. Louis P. Roberts, Proprietor." Demolished.

Newport's Beautiful Cliff Walk, Newport, R.I. c. 1905.

The New Cliff Hotel, Newport, R.I. c. 1906. Demolished.

Newport, R.I. Along the Cliff Walk, North. c. 1905. Note, no jogging attire here—rather we see white parasols, children in suits, and ladies with fancy hats. The lady in the foreground is holding on to her hat, implying a stiff breeze on the Walk that day.

The Forty Steps, Cliff Walk, Newport, R.I. c. 1906. Today the steps are stone, part of a community restoration effort. You can see the Breakers in the back upper right of the image.

Forty Steps, Newport, R.I. c. 1906. In the margin is written: "Wouldn't you like to climb these steps! Will write soon. Have been away two weeks but is seems like two days, it has gone so quickly. Gertrude."

Cliffs from Forty Steps, Newport, R.I. c. 1910.

Newport, R.I. Cliff Walk showing the Breakers. c. 1909.

Cliff Walk Showing the Breakers, Newport, R.I. c. 1910. Ochre Court is shown on the right, with The Breakers in the distance. The first tunnel is shown in this card. On the back is printed: *Cliff Walk showing the "Breakers," Newport, R.I. The Cliff Walk is the most beautiful walk in the world. Beginning at the western end of Newport Beach, it winds in and out along the rocky cliffs for three miles, passing through some of the most beautiful estates in this country and ending at Spouting Rock Beach.*

Vanderbilt Mansion—Ogden Goelet / Along the shore of Cliff Walk, south from Forty Steps, Newport, Rhode Island. c. 1930.

Along famous Cliff Walk, Newport, R.I. c. 1930.

Cliff Walks, Newport, R.I. c. 1910.

Tunnel on Cliff Walk, Newport, R.I. c. 1912. Hand written note on the back: "Friend John: Your card was received and was glad to here [sic] from you. There is some pretty nice scenery up here to paint but I am a little busy now. Regards to all. Ed."

Cliff Walk. c. 1914.

Vanderbilt Estate "The Breakers" and Ogden Goelet's Estate from Cliff Walk, Newport, R.I. c.1910.

Ogden Goelet, Villa Ochre, Newport, R.I. c. 1905.

Ochre Court, Residence of Ogden Goelet, Newport, R.I. c. 1906. Printed on the back: *Situated on the Cliff Walk, near the "Breakers." One of the show places of Newport.*

Hamilton MacKay Tombley Residence Ochre Point Ave., Newport, R.I. c. 1910. This view is of the front of the home, not the Cliff Walk side.

The Breakers, Newport, R.I. c. 1910. Vanderbilt had gates erected on either side of the Walk past his property. They were for decoration and were never locked.

"The Breakers" Mrs. Cornelius Vanderbilt's Residence, Newport, R.I. As with many Newport postcards, mansion owners' names often list the wife as the owner.

Newport, R.I. Cliff Walk (Ragged Cliffs). c. 1910. Note The Breakers' gates at the end of the white walk.

Seal Rock, Along Cliff Walk, Newport c.1950. Forty-five years later than the previous card.

Newport, R.I. The Cliff Walk from "The Breakers." c. 1905. Hand written in the margins: "8/25/1905 The real walk is much better than the picture. This is a rainy day and the talk is more important than the rain."

Cliff Walk, Ochre Point, Newport, R.I. c. 1907. This view is of the far gates on the Breakers' property, showing the Drexel residence through the fence.

Ochre Point, Along Cliff Walk, Newport, R.I. c. 1932. Looking back at the gate to the entrance of The Breakers.

Ochre Point, Along Cliff Walk, Newport, R.I. c. 1950. The same view as the previous card, almost two decades later.

Cliff Walk, Newport, R.I. c. 1905. Written in the margin: "Dear Fan-Your letter was forwarded to me-How short! Talk about Saratoga! You sh'd see this-Whew! Sally."

John R. Drexel's Residence, Cliff Walk, Newport, R.I. c. 1910.

Residences Along Cliff Walk from Belmont Beach, Newport Rhode Island – T.S. Taylor – C. Ogden Jones – J.R. Drexel. c. 1950.

Residences along Cliff Walk, Most beautiful walk in the World, Newport, Rhode Island. c. 1950.

Residences of C. Ogden Jones, J.R. Drexel, and F. Pearson, Ochre Point, Newport, R.I. c. 1912.

The Cliff Walk, Newport, R.I. c. 1909. Hand written note: "Our vacation will soon be over. I hope you had a nice time also that you have all been well. Newport is a beautiful place. I should like very much to live here. Tim."

Ochre Point, Cliff Walk Newport, R.I. c. 1910.

Ochre Point, Newport, R.I. c. 1910.

Foot of Marine Ave. Cliff Walk, Newport, R.I. c. 1908.

Cliff Walk, Newport, R.I. c. 1910.

"Seaview Terrace," Residence of Edson Bradley, Newport, R.I. c. 1940.

The Cliffs, North, Newport, R.I.
c. 1909.

Mrs. H.P. Whitney's Studio. Cliff Walk, Newport, R.I.
c.1915. Destroyed in a 1938 hurricane and rebuilt. Whitney, a daughter of Cornelius Vanderbilt II, was a sculptor; among other things, she founded the Whitney Museum in New York.

Rosecliff Residence of Herman Oelrich, Newport, R.I. c. 1906. On the reverse is printed: *Rosecliff, Res. of Herman Oelrich. Newport, R.I. Faces the Cliff Walk and Bellevue Ave. One of Newport's beautiful residences.*

Along Cliff Walk, South from Estate of Perry Belmont, Newport, R.I. c. 1910. The hand written note states: "Call in about 10am tomorrow and I will show you the original of view in opposite side of card. With fondest wishes Mrs. Green." The third structure from the right is The Breakers (in the far distance).

Beechwood, Newport, R.I. Residence of John Jacob Astor. c. 1910.

Marble Palace, Mrs. O.H. P. Belmont's House, Newport, R.I. c.1906.

Japanese Tea House. Estate of Mrs. O.H.P. Belmont, Newport, R.I. c. 1928. Most postcards are postmarked in the summer months.

Newport, R.I. Cliff Walk from Marble Palace. c. 1908. Sent by Jennie B. Tripp, who lived at 17 Bull Street in Newport, on September 28, 1908.

The Tunnel, Cliff Walk, Newport, R.I. c.1910.

The Tunnel in Cliff, Newport, R.I. c. 1908.

TUNNEL ON CLIFF WALK, NEWPORT, R.I.

Tunnel on Cliff Walk, Newport, R.I. c.1910.

The Arch, Cliff Walk, showing Tea House in Distance, Newport, R.I. c. 1919.

"Miramir," Residence of Dr. A. Hamilton Rice, Newport, R.I. c. 1950.

Residence of F. Lathrop Ames, Along Cliff Walk, Newport, R.I. c. 1952. Hand written note on back: "Guess you are very lucky in not getting much snow in these coastal blizzards we have had so many of but the Cape is worse off than we here so am glad we are here. What do you think of the Greyhound strike out West? R."

View of Rough Point, along Cliff Walk, Newport, R.I. c. 1919.

Along Beautiful Cliff Walk, Newport, R.I. c. 1950. Rough Point is the last house on the left.

F.W. Vanderbilt's Residence, Rough Point, Newport, R.I. c. 1905. Showing the original state of the mansion.

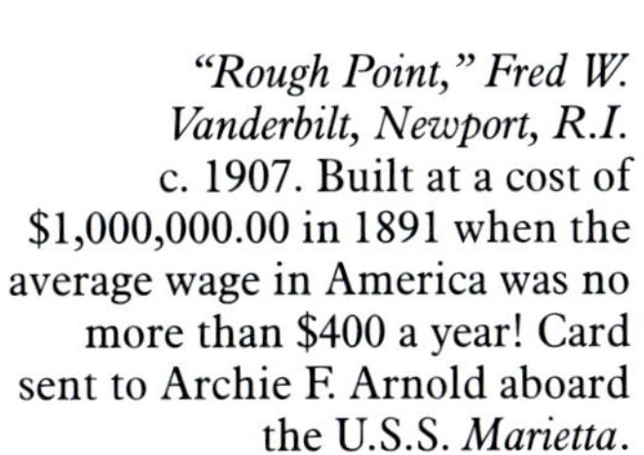

"Rough Point," Fred W. Vanderbilt, Newport, R.I. c. 1907. Built at a cost of $1,000,000.00 in 1891 when the average wage in America was no more than $400 a year! Card sent to Archie F. Arnold aboard the U.S.S. *Marietta*.

Rough Point, W.B. Leed's Residence, Newport, R.I. c. 1915.

Along the Cliff Walk, Livingstone Beekman Residence, Newport, R.I. c. 1906.

C. Warren Lippitt Residence, Newport, R.I. c. 1911.

Newport, R.I. The Castle Ex. Gov. Lippet's [sic] Res. c. 1909.

Along the Cliff Walk. Bailey's Beach in Distance, Newport, R.I. c. 1906.

MR. CLARENCE DOLAN'S RESIDENCE, BELLEVUE AVE., NEWPORT, R. I. 10962

Mr. Clarence Dolan's Residence, Bellevue Ave., Newport, R.I. c. 1910. Lippitt's Castle on the right.

The Cliffs, from Bailey's Beach, Newport, R.I. c.1911. Hand written message to Jennie C. Caswell: "I would like very much to exchange photo's with you, that is if you are willing. I think it would be nice to see what each other looks like. Ans. soon."

The Cliffs from Bailey's Beach, Newport, R.I. c. 1909. The moon could never come up over this spot, but it looks good, so the card's publisher added a romantic touch!

Newport, R.I. Bailey's Beach. View from the Cliff Walk. c. 1909.

Cliff Walk Looking Towards Bailey's Beach, Newport, R.I. c. 1912.

Newport, R.I. Bailey's Beach, where the 400 bathe. C. 1910.

Bailey's Beach, Newport, R.I. c. 1950.

Bailey's Beach, Newport, R.I. c. 1950.

Chapter Two

Newport Mansions

Driving or walking down Bellevue Avenue today (and overlooking a very few modern architectural mistakes), one is taken back in time to the turn of the twentieth century. The mansions of "America's Royalty" stand today as sentinels to power and wealth, unprecedented in our nation's history. One masterpiece after another lines the Avenue, showcasing some of America's finest architectural designs.

At the turn of the century, only two classes of people gained entrance: the wealthy or the servants. Today, admission for over a dozen of these monuments to power is by prepaid ticket, purchased by hundreds of thousands of tourists each year. Newport's finest hour lives on in these restored mansions. We picture here the more popular and ostentatious of the "cottages," as illustrated on postcards purchased during Newport's Gilded Age by tourists who would never see the insides of these mansions. They were limited at that time to a glimpse from the street of the wealth that built Bellevue Avenue.

During the Gilded Age, the average salary in the U.S. was around $400.00 per year. In Newport, however, it was not unusual for a villa to rent for between $3,000.00 and $12,000.00 for the season—which consisted of just three months. Property taxes also varied dramatically in Newport. Taxes for a very modest Newport home ranged from $15.00 to no more than $125.00 a year. In contrast, Avenue homes such as Chateau-sur-Mer or The Elms were assessed at between $7,500.00 and $10,000.00 in annual taxes.

Opposite Page:
This map of the Newport mansions was produced in the 1930s as a tourist brochure. It shows in detail drawings of the mansions and their owners at the time. Copyright 1933, by the Mount Hope Bridge Corporation, Bristol, Rhode Island.

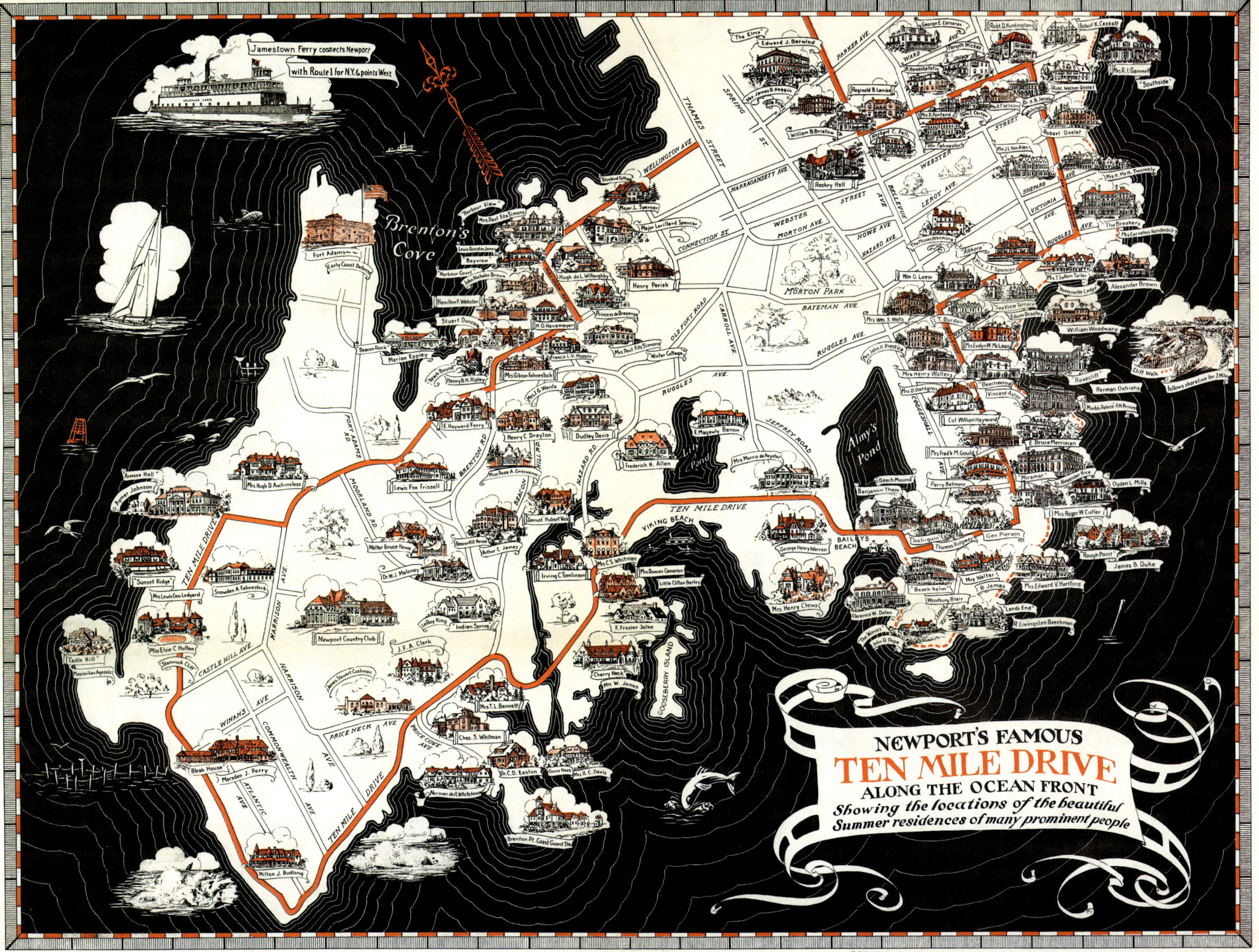
NEWPORT'S FAMOUS
TEN MILE DRIVE
ALONG THE OCEAN FRONT
Showing the locations of the beautiful Summer residences of many prominent people
Jamestown Ferry connects Newport
with Route 1 for N.Y. & points West
Brenton's Cove
Fort Adams
Early Coast Defense
Almy's Pond
Lily Pond
Morton Park
Gooseberry Island
Thames Street
Spring St.
Bellevue Ave.
Narragansett Ave.
Webster
Morton Ave.
Connection St.
Wellington Ave.
Old Fort Road
Carroll Ave.
Bateman Ave.
Ruggles Ave.
Jeffrey Road
Ten Mile Drive
Viking Beach
Bailey's Beach
Coggeshall Ave.
Harrison Ave.
Castle Hill Ave.
Winans Ave.
Commonwealth Ave.
Atlantic Ave.
Price Neck Ave.
Price Cove Ave.
Moorland Rd.
Brenton Rd.
Fort Adams Rd.
Hazard Rd.
Beacon Hill Rd.
Newport Country Club
"Castle Hill"
"Sunset Ridge"
Bleak House
Milton J. Budlong
Marsden J. Perry
Brenton Pt. Coast Guard Sta.
Chas. S. Whitman
Mrs. T. L. Bennett
Dr. C. D. Easton
J. F. A. Clark
Indian Spring
Irving C. Tomlinson
F. Frazier Jelke
Cherry Neck
Mrs. W. James
Mrs. Henry Clews
George Henry Warren
Mrs. Hugh D. Auchincloss
Lewis Fox Frissell
Henry C. Drayton
Dudley Davis
Frederick H. Allen
E. Hayward Ferry
Walter Bruce Howe
Snowden A. Fahnestock
Miss Elsie C. Hutton
Henry Parish
H. O. Havemeyer
Marion Eppley
Beacon Rock
Rocky Hall
William B. Bristow
Edward J. Berwind
"The Elms"
Robert Goelet
The Breakers
Mrs. Cornelius Vanderbilt
Alexander Brown
William Woodward
Rosecliff
Herman Oelrichs
Marble Palace - O.H. Belmont
Vincent Astor
"Beechwood"
Col. William Hayward
E. Bruce Merriman
Miramar
Ogden L. Mills
Mrs. Roger W. Cutler
Rough Point
James B. Duke
Mrs. Edward V. Hartford
Lands End
R. Livingston Beeckman
Beech Mound
Benjamin Thaw
Perry Belmont
Gen Pierson
Cliff Walk
follows shoreline for 3 Miles
"Southside"
Lithographed in U. S. A.
COPYRIGHT. 1933. BY MOUNT HOPE BRIDGE CORPORATION. BRISTOL. RHODE ISLAND

E.J. Berwind's Residence, Newport, R.I. c. 1907. (The Elms) Completed in 1901 at a cost of $1,400,000.00. Designed by Horace Trumbauer, copying Chateau d'Asnieres outside Paris. Mrs. Berwind died in 1922 and Mr. Berwind in 1936. He made his money in coal. His sister Julia lived in the mansion until 1961. Owned by the Preservation Society of Newport County and open for tours.

"The Elms." Fountain and Gardens, Estate of E.J. Berwind, Newport, R.I. c. 1910.

The Elms, Newport, R.I. Residence of E.J. Berwind. c. 1907. Back view of card # 1.

Villa Rosa, Residence of Mr. E. Rollins Morse, Newport, R.I. c. 1920. Demolished.

Villa of Dr. Barton Jacobs, Newport, R.I. c.1912. Showing the back of the mansion. Demolished for dormitories for Salve University. Mrs. Jacobs' former husband was Robert Garrett, President of the Baltimore and Ohio Railroad. He believed himself to be the Prince of Wales and his wife hired actors to impersonate court officials to support his delusion. His favorite court character was The Crown Prince of Germany, played by Newport's Harry Lehr.

Residence of Dr. Barton Jacobs, Newport, R.I. c. 1912. Street view.

Dr. Barton Jacobs, Residence, Newport, R.I. c. 1919. Front view. Printed on the back: *Narragansett Avenue, near "Forty Steps." A beautiful residence that should be seen to be fully appreciated.*

Robert Goelet's Residence, Newport, R.I. c. 1914.

"The Orchard", Residence of Mr. George R. Fearing Newport, R.I. c. 1915.

Residence of Mr. Wm. Gammell, Newport, R.I. c. 1915. Demolished.

The R.I. Gammell Estate. Newport, R.I. c. 1915. Demolished.

Residence of Mrs. T. Shaw Safe, Newport, R.I. c. 1912. The story goes that when Mrs. Stuyvesant Fish was introduced to Mr. Shaw-Safe, she addressed him as Mr. Safe, he corrected her and Mrs. Fish responded that she couldn't remember the *combination* of his name.

"Ochre Court," Residence of Mrs. Ogden Golet [sic], Newport, R.I. c. 1906. In 1946, Mr. Goelet offered this 100-room mansion to his daughter, who was attending Vassar; she refused the mansion, stating that the thought of living there "oppressed" her. In 1947, Goelet gave Ochre Court to the Catholic Church. Today it is used as the administration building for Salve University.

Residence of Ogden Goelet, Cliff Walk, Newport, R.I. c. 1906. Rear view. The view from the Cliff Walk today is almost identical to this card.

"Wakehurst" summer villa of James. J. Van Allen, Newport, R.I. c. 1910.

Residence of J.J. Van Allen, Newport, R.I. c. 1910. Wakehurst. Built by Dudley Newton from plans by C.E. Kempe.

Newport, R.I. J.J. Van Allen's Sunken Gardens. c. 1908. Gardens of the two previous cards.

(on the back is printed) *The Baptist Home of Rhode Island, Shepard Avenue, Newport, R.I.* c. 1950s. Hand written message: "This picture isn't too good but you can get some idea. There will be 54 rooms when it is all complete. Lots to be done yet, Bye now, Grace." Known as The Watts Sherman House and designed by Henry Hobson Richardson, it is the only surviving example of Richardson's work in Newport. Built for one of the Wetmore daughters, Anne, on adjoining property to Château-sur-Mer. Owned by Salve University and not open to the public.

Mrs. H. McK. Twombly Residence, Newport, R.I. c. 1912. Originally built in 1883 and designed by Peabody and Stearns. Called Vinland. Catherine Lorillard Wolfe sold the mansion to the Twomblys in 1896. Wolfe was the sister of Pierre Lorillard, who built the original Breakers that burned in 1892. Vinland is owned by Salve Regina University today.

Residence of H. McKay Trombley [sic], Newport, R.I. c. 1912. Cliff Walk view of the previous card. Note the different color to the stone. It is not unusual for postcards of the same building to have different unrealistic colors.

The Breakers, Newport, R.I. c. 1906. Front view of the mansion. Built in 1895 and designed by Richard Morris Hunt, it contains seventy rooms in the Italian Renaissance style. Cornelius Vanderbilt II bought the original Breakers in 1885 and commissioned Hunt to design the new Breakers after a fire destroyed the original mansion. Hunt died in 1896. The estate was bequeathed by Mrs. Cornelius Vanderbilt to her niece, the Countess Szechenyi, wife of the Austro-Hungarian charge d'affaires to the United States in 1906. Today it is owned by The Newport Preservation Society and open to the public. It is the Society's most visited mansion, with hundreds of thousands of visitors each year.

Cornelius Vanderbilt House, Newport, R.I. c. 1906. Cliff Walk view of previous card.

"The Breakers" Cliff View, Newport, R.I. c. 1910. Another Cliff Walk view.

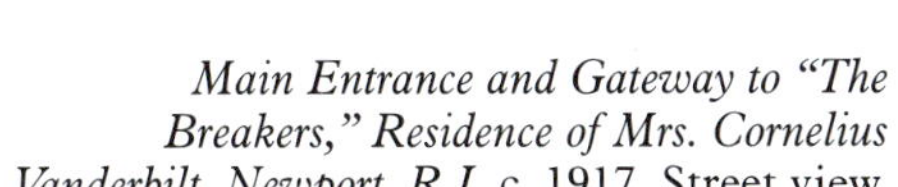
Main Entrance and Gateway to "The Breakers," Residence of Mrs. Cornelius Vanderbilt, Newport, R.I. c. 1917. Street view.

The Playhouse at The Breakers, Newport, Rhode Island. c. 1950s. Printed on the back: *Children's Playhouse at "The Breakers," Cornelius Vanderbilt Residence, Newport, R.I. Open under the auspices of the Preservation Society of Newport County*. The Playhouse was designed by Peabody and Stearns in 1886.

Mid Cliff, George D. Widener, Newport, R.I. c.1924. Photo cards such as this one generally sell for about double the price of standard non photo cards, as there were fewer printed.

Commodore Baldwin's House, Newport, R.I. c. 1911. Called Ivy Lodge.

Residence of J. R. Drexel, Newport, R. I.

Residence of J.R. Drexel, Newport, R.I. c. 1905. Today, this mansion is not recognizable and is called Fairholme.

"Mid-Cliff" C. Ogden M. Jones Residence, Ochre Point, Newport, R.I. c. 1905.

Edison Bradley Estate, Newport, Rhode Island. c. 1950. Called Sea View Terrace, designed by architect Howard Greenley. Bradley was the President of the Kentucky Distilling Company. His principal home was at Dupont Circle in Washington, D.C.; he purchased Sea View in 1923. Bradley died along with the stock market crash in 1929. Currently used by Salve Regina University for student residences and classrooms. Called Carey Mansion by the New York family that still owns it.

Ocher Point and the Cliff Walk, Newport, R.I. (from left to right) "Mason Lea" Mrs. Geo. W. Collard, "The Breakers" Mrs. Cornelius Vanderbilt, "Mid Cliff" Mrs.C. Ogden Jones, "Fairholm" John R. Drexel, "Anglesea" Mrs. Frederick Pearson. c. 1915. The gazebo is no longer in existence. Mid Cliff was the home of Perle Mesta, "the hostess with the mostest."

Residence of Senator Wetmore, Newport, R.I. c. 1905. Additional view of previous card.

Senator Geo. P. Wetmore's Residence Newport, R.I. c. 1905. Called "Château-sur-Mer" and built in 1852 by China trade merchant William Shepard Wetmore. In 1857, he held a "Fete Champetre" for two thousand guests here. He died in 1862. His son George Peabody Wetmore inherited the mansion when he was sixteen and waited seven years before remodeling the home. It was remodeled in the 1870s under the direction of architect Richard Morris Hunt in the Second Empire style. Senator Wetmore died in 1921 and left the mansion to his two daughters, Edith and Maude, who never married. The Preservation Society of Newport purchased the mansion in 1969 and it is open to the public today. Much of the original furnishings are intact.

"Chetwood [sic]," Residence of J.J. Astor, Newport, R.I. c. 1950s. "Chetwode," built for William Storrs Wells on the northeast corner of Bellevue and Ruggles around 1900. Demolished in 1973.

Newport, R.I. Residence of Richard Gambrell's c. 1910. Designed by architect Thomas Hastings with the firm of Carrère & Hastings. Called "Vernon Court." Allard was contracted for interiors. Presently serves as the National Museum of American Illustration.

Asbestos "Century" Shingles / Applied French Method on the Residence of Geo. S. Scott, Newport, Rhode Island. c. 1910. An advertising card promoting asbestos shingles. One wonders if the property owner received a discount for the promotion. In the 1930s, this was the home of Mrs. John H. Prentice.

"Rosecliff," Residence of Mrs. Herman Oelrichs, front view from Bellevue, Ave., Newport, R.I. c. 1905. Note the early automobile at the front of the house. Inspired by the Grand Trianon of Louis XVI at Versailles, this home was built between 1897-1902. Architect McKim, Mead & White. Tessie (Theresa Fair) Oelrichs was an heir to the Comstock Load silver fortune; Herman owned ocean liners. Tessie ran "Rosecliff" like a drill sergeant—she had the bed linens changed daily and if the marble floors weren't cleaned to her satisfaction, she got down on the floor and scrubbed them herself. She was also known for her famous "White Ball," where guests were all in white and the ballroom decorated in white. In a freak accident at "Rosecliff," Tessie was blinded in one eye by a falling tack. She lost her mind in the end and wandered her marble palace, fragile but still beautiful, asking imaginary guests to have just one more glass of champagne. Today, Rosecliff is owned by the Preservation Society of Newport and open to the public.

E.C. Knight Residence, Newport, R.I. c. 1911. Built in 1904, architect Horace Trumbauer. Mansion is called "Clarendon Court." Edward Collings Knight was a Pennsylvania Railroad magnate. The name "Clarendon Court" came from the original name "Claradon Court," which in turn came from the first name of Knight's wife, Clara.

Residence of Mr. E.C. Knight of Philadelphia, Newport, R.I. c. 1905. Showing the rear view of the mansion.

The Porch of the Residence of Mr. E.C. Knight, Newport, R.I. c. 1905. These gardens no long exist in this form.

By-The-Sea, Residence of Hon. Perry Belmont, Bellevue Ave., Newport, R.I. c.1906. Built in 1860. Architect George Champlin Mason Sr., the most important architect in Newport during the 1860s. Demolished.

Residence of Harry Payne Whitney, Newport, R.I. c. 1922. Called "The Reefs," "Sea-Cliffe," and The Christopher Wolfe house through the years. The architect was Joseph Collins Wells and the home was built in the Italian Villa style between 1852 and 1853. It was located north of Rosecliff. Whitney purchased the house in the early 1920s and called it "Whitney Cottage." Burned in 1942.

Beechwood, Residence of Mrs. Wm. Astor, Newport, R.I. c. 1905. Built in 1851 for merchant Daniel Parrish and ended up in the hands of Mrs. Caroline Backhouse Astor. Architect was Calvert Vaux with landscaping by Andrew Jackson Downing. Additions by Architect William Morris Hunt in the 1890s. Mrs. Astor, titled "The Mystic Rose," died in 1908. In *The Last Resort*, Cleveland Amory writes that "in her last years, Mrs. Astor's mind failed. Her final summers at Beechwood were spent in solitary splendor, still erect, still bravely gowned and jeweled, she stood quite alone, greeting imaginary guests long dead, exchanging pleasantries with ghosts of the utmost social distinction." Today, Beechwood is open to the public as a house museum operated by The Beechwood Foundation.

"Ball Room" Beechwood, Mrs. William Astor, Newport, R.I. c. 1907. William Morris Hunt was commissioned by Mr. Astor to design this ballroom. A year after this card was mailed, Mrs. Astor was dead.

Marble Palace Built by W.K. Vanderbilt, Newport, R.I. c. 1909. Written Feb, 3, 1909: "Dear Uncle Frank, Thank you very much for the post-card you sent me. I have been collecting them for three years now, but I only have about six hundred. It has been very cold up here for the past three or four weeks, at least the temperature fell to four degrees below zero. As the river is frozen over, you sometimes see an ice boat out on it. Aff. Robert Storer." Marble House was built between 1888 and 1892 for Mr. and Mrs. William K. Vanderbilt. $11,000,000.00, later Newport had one of its most striking "cottages." It was designed by Richard Morris Hunt with inspiration from Versailles' Petit Trianon. Divorced in 1895, Alva Vanderbilt married a friend and neighbor down the street, O.H.P. Belmont, and moved in with him. After Belmont's death, Alva moved back into Marble House and had The Chinese Tea House built on the edge of the Cliff Walk. Marble House is owned today by the Preservation Society of Newport County and open for tours.

Marble Palace, Mrs. Belmont's Residence. Newport, R.I. c. 1910. After working with soup kitchens, birth control, and poor clinics, the energetic and socially conscious Alva turned to the women's suffrage movement. Marble House was soon hosting conclaves of suffragettes. Alva was overheard to say to a young lady at one of the meetings at Marble House: "Brace up my dear, just pray to God. She will help you." Alva's end was in Paris at the age of eighty in 1933.

The Marble Palace, Residence of Mrs. O.H.P. Belmont, Newport, R.I. c. 1909. Alva was Newport's "Queen of the Firsters." As a "cottager,'" she was the first to ride a bicycle in bloomers, first to have an automobile, first woman elected to the American Institute of Architects, one of the first to cut off her hair shoulder length, and in 1895 she got a divorce—something just not done! The grounds for divorce: adultery!

Japanese Tea House, Estate of Mrs. O.H.P. Belmont, Newport, R.I. c. 1912. The Tea House was built to extraordinary detail, with one exception: there was no way to make tea in it! Finding out, Alva had a miniature railroad built from the mansion kitchen out to the tea house. Footed livery held silver trays over their heads while squatting inside the miniature cars.

Residence of Pembroke Jones, Newport, R.I. c. 1917. On the back is printed: *Residence of Pembroke Jones, Newport, R.I. Situated on Bellevue Avenue. One of Newport's beautiful residences.* Pembroke Jones used to set aside $300,000.00 at the beginning of every season for entertainment extras—this at a time when the average U.S. wage was $400.00 a year!

Italian Garden. Estate of Dr. Hamilton Rice, Newport, R.I. c. 1950. Also called *The Mrs. George D. Widener House.* Finished in 1914, architect Horace Trumbauer. Mrs. Widener's husband and son died on the *Titanic* in 1912 during the construction of Miramar. Mrs. Widener married Dr. Alexander Hamilton Rice and the couple sponsored the annual Tennis Week Ball, which became a great Newport tradition. Today this is a private residence.

Newport, R.I. Residence of Oliver Hazard Perry Belmont. c. 1909. Built between 1891-1894, architect was Richard Morris Hunt. This card shows the original entrance façade. The rear of the mansion faces Bellevue Avenue—does that make a statement! O.H.P. Belmont loved horses. (He founded the Belmont Racetrack.) His father owned By-The-Sea, a cottage on Bellevue Avenue. The first floor stored horses and carriages and Belmont had quarters on the second story. Alva Vanderbilt's move to Belcourt kicked out the horses and the first floor was then devoted to entertainment. After Belmont's death in 1908, Alva remodeled Belcourt into a somewhat more fashionable Bellevue Avenue "cottage," finally deciding to move across the street back to Marble House. Belcourt is now owned by Donald and Harley Tinney and the mansion is open as a house museum.

Residence of F. Lathrop Ames, Along Cliff Walk, Newport, R.I. c. 1920s. In the 1930s, it was listed as the home of Mrs. Roger. W. Cutler and called Rock Cliff.

Rough Point, Residence of Wm. B. Leeds, Newport, R.I. c. 1920. Printed on the back: *Rough Point, Res. of Wm. B. Leeds, Newport, R.I. Situated on the Cliff Walk near Ledge Road near Lippett's Castle. One of Newport's Show Places.* Leeds was known in Newport as "The Tinplate King." He would laughingly relate that his wife could never keep to her $40,000.00 a year dress allowance.

ROUGH POINT, RESIDENCE OF WM. B. LEEDS, NEWPORT, R. I.

Residence of F.W. Vanderbilt, Bellevue Avenue, Newport, R.I. c. 1907. Architect Peabody & Stearns. Finished in 1891 at a cost of $1,000,000.00.

The Duke Estate, Newport, R.I. c. 1930s. Duke purchased Rough Point in 1922. He hired architect Horace Trumbauer to modify and enlarge the mansion. Daughter Doris inherited the home in 1925 and used it until she passed away in the late twentieth century. Owned today by The Newport Restoration Foundation and open as a house museum, virtually intact as Ms. Duke left it.

Residence of J.R. Drexel, Cliff Walk, Newport, R.I. c. 1908. This card is mislabeled. The name should read H. Mortimer Brooks. Demolished.

"Aspen Hall" John Aspegren's Residence, Newport, R.I. c. 1929. Written on the back: "Dearest Mother, This is one of the many wonderful houses on Ocean Drive. The flowers were simply wonderful. Love Gillie." The Aspegrens' introduction to Newport Society was via their first party; toward the end of the evening, when guests were ready to move on (to another party), an enormous amount of activity took place on the lawn, with a hundred men assembling staging and lights to reveal that the Russian Ballet had been shipped in from New York City to perform for the crowd. All stayed for the rest of the evening. Demolished.

The Castle from Cliff Walk, Residence of Charles Warren Lippett [sic], Newport, R.I. c. 1910. Printed on the back: *Situated on the Cliff, built on the stern. Severe lines of an old English Castle.* Was located on Ledge Road right on the Cliff Walk; also called Norman Castle and on some postcards called The Breakwater. Demolished to make way for the construction of The Waves, home of John R. Pope.

Chas. Lippets [sic] House, Newport, R.I. c. 1912. Poetic license was taken here: the moon could never come up in this position.

Beachmond, Residence of Benjamin Thaw, Newport, R.I. c. 1910. Printed on the back of the card: *Situated on Bellevue Avenue, near Bailey's Beach. One of Newport's beautiful residences.* Built between 1897-1898 and located at the corner of Bellevue and Ocean Drive. Architect Henry Ives Cobb. Thaw was a Pittsburgh banker and philanthropist.

"The Rocks" Henry Clews Residence, Newport, R.I. c. 1906. Shell decorated cards tend to have double the value of ordinary Newport postcards. Mrs. Henry Clews was the grand-niece of Dolly Madison and was Newport's best-dressed lady. She set aside $10,000.00 a season for "mistakes" in her clothes. Demolished.

Mr. Henry Clews, "The Rocks" Newport, R.I. c. 1906.

Indian Spring, The Busk Residence, Newport, R.I. c. 1914. Built between 1889-1892. Architect Richard Morris Hunt. Later known as Wrentham House. Originally contracted for William E. Dorsheimer, Lieutenant-Governor of New York, but his death in 1888 stopped the construction. Joseph Busk continued with the construction and had the mansion finished. A private home today.

Along the Ocean Drive. Residences of Mr. Olmstead, Mrs. Busk and Mr. Rawson. Newport, R.I. c. 1910.

"Crossways" Residence of Mrs. Stuyvesant Fish. Newport, R.I. c. 1910. Built between 1897-1898. Architect Dudley Newton. Furnishings by Newport's Vernon Co. Fifteen servants kept Crossways going, a rather small number by Newport standards, though Fish's staff problems rarely kept servants over a year. Mrs. Fish never finished school, couldn't spell, and seldom read even a newspaper, but she was the third member of Newport's "Great Triumvirate," which also included Mrs. Oelrichs and Mrs. Belmont.

"Cherry Neck" Residence of Mrs. Wortham James, Ocean Drive, Newport, R.I. c. 1940s. Also called Normandie. Built in 1914. Architect William Adams Delano.

Newport Country Club, Newport, R.I. c. 1915. Built 1894-1895. Architect Whitney Warren. Warren also designed Grand Central Station in New York and the Biltmore Hotel in Providence. In addition, he designed a hotel complex for James Gordon Bennett, to be added onto Bennett's Stone Villa, located across from the Casino on Bellevue Avenue. The hotel complex was never built.

Golf Club House, Newport, R.I. c. 1905.

Interior Newport Country Club, Newport, R.I. c. 1910.

"Bleak House" Residence of Mardsen J. Perry, Newport, R.I. c. 1910. A self-made multimillionaire, Perry was the executive of a local electric company and president of a bank. He also had one of the most impressive collections of eighteenth century furniture, all sold after his death. His Providence home is today the Rhode Island Historical Society. Demolished.

T. M. Davis Residence, Breton Point, Newport, R.I. c. 1912. Known as the Budlong Estate. Site at Brenton State Park on Ocean Drive. Demolished.

Gateway and Porter's Lodge, "Shamrock Cliff" G.M. Hutton. Newport, R.I. c. 1907. Built between 1894-1896. Architect Peabody & Stearns. Commissioned by Irish Diplomat Gaun McRobert Hutton. Today, this is a time-share and hotel.

"Shamrock Cliff" Residence of G.M. Hutton, Newport, R.I. c. 1910.

Residence of Mr. Charles F. Hoffman of New York, Newport, R.I. c. 1910. Demolished.

"Vedimar," L.F. Frissell, Newport, R.I. c. 1929. Demolished.

Residence of Commodore James, Newport, R.I. c. 1938. Called Beacon Hill House. James owned copper companies. Demolished.

The Blue Gardens, Arthur Curtis James Estate, Newport, R.I. c. 1940s.

Swiss Village, Commodore James Estate, Newport, R.I. c. 1920s. The Swiss Village was designed in the manner of Marie Antoinette's Petit Hameau at Versailles. Around fifty picturesque buildings were constructed, along winding paths to duplicate a Swiss village. The farm had a menagerie of animals, with the pigs having their own yard and sty. The listing of animals each had its own signboard displayed in verse. Several of the buildings are still standing.

Residence of William Grosvenor, Newport, R.I. c. 1915.

"Beacon Rock" (E.D. Morgan's Residence), Newport, R.I. c. 1909. Built between 1888-1891. Architect McKim, Mead & White. The house was named after the promontory Beacon Rock, with the final design and sighting looking somewhat like the Acropolis.

E. D. Morgan's House and Harbor, Newport, R.I. c. 1910.

Harbor Court, Estate of Mrs. John Nicholas Brown, Newport, R.I. c. 1910. Built between 1903-1905. Architect Cram, Ferguson & Goodhue. Built at a cost of $103,000.00 for recent widow Natalie Bayard Brown. Sold to the New York Yacht Club in 1987 for their Newport headquarters.

Boat Landing of Commodore James Estate and Marion Eppley Estate, Newport, R.I. c. 1915.

Residence of John N. Brown, Newport, R.I. c. 1915.

Residence of Mrs. A.S. Clarke, Newport, R.I. c. 1915. Called Beachbound. Built 1895 for William Burden. Architect Peabody & Stearns.

Harbor View (Mrs. F.O. French's Residence), Newport, R.I. c. 1906. Demolished.

Residence of Lorillard Spencer, Newport, R.I. c. 1911.

August Belmont Memorial Chapel, Newport, R.I. c. 1910.

St. Joseph's House convent of the Cenacle, *Newport, R.I.* c. 1930s.

Residence of Louis Bruguiere, Newport, R.I. c. 1914. Demolished.

White Hall Residence of J.J. Coogan, Newport, R.I. c. 1915. Architect Stanford White. A fire gutted Whitehall soon after the Coogan family moved in and they never returned, allowing the mansion to continue crumbling for thirty-five years, until two years before Mrs. Coogan's death. It was torn down in 1945.

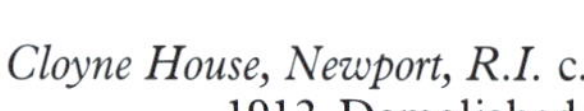

Cloyne House, Newport, R.I. c. 1912. Demolished.

Chapter Three

Bellevue Avenue

Gilded Age society had firmly established itself by the turn of the century in Newport, characterized by palatial mansions, fancy balls, and a social life unheard of across America. To support the extravagances of the ultra rich, the already established Bellevue shopping and entertainment area provided the goods and services to those who could afford luxury items and services. Much of the Bellevue Avenue shopping area remains intact today, just as it appeared in turn-of-the-century postcards.

Famous architects designed the buildings, starting at Memorial Boulevard on Bellevue. Travers Block, for example, was designed by Richard Morris Hunt and built in the Stick Style between 1870 and 1871. The Audrain Building's architect was Bruce Price. The Casino was designed by McKim, Mead and White in 1879-81 and commissioned by James Gordon Bennett (of *New York Herald* newspaper money). The Casino was created to provide an entertainment center for the wealthy—a country club. Tennis courts, a billiard parlor, a bowling alley, a theater, a restaurant, and shops provided venues for dog and horse shows, parties, and a place to see and be seen. Today, this shopping area is alive and well, housing the American Tennis Hall of Fame plus restaurants and fine shops.

Casino and Bellevue Ave., Newport, R.I. c.1907. Showing the intersection of Bellevue with the Travers Block on the left of the card. Travers Block was built between 1870-1871 and designed by architect Richard Morris Hunt. When built, it comprised the largest block of shops in Newport. A thriving business block exists today on the corner of Bellevue and Memorial Blvd.

Bellevue Avenue, Newport, R.I. c. 1910. This card shows the view a little further back than the previous card.

The Casino, Newport, R.I. c. 1907. The Casino was built between 1879-1881. Architect McKim, Meade & White. Commissioned by James Gordon Bennett, Jr., this was the center of Newport life. It is still standing today and the home of the Newport Tennis Hall of Fame.

Bellevue Avenue, Newport, R.I. c. 1915. Showing mostly the Casino.

Casino, Bellevue Avenue, Looking South, Newport, R.I. c. 1922. Notice the mix of automobiles and horse drawn carriages on this card. During the season, the Casino published programs through the summer. A schedule of events was listed for morning, afternoon, and evening concerts, performances at the Casino Theatre, the National Lawn Tennis Tournament, the Newport Horse Show, and the Newport Dog Show. Many of these programs are archived in the library of the Preservation Society of Newport County.

Casino and Bellevue Ave., Newport, R.I. c. 1908.

Newport, R.I. The Casino. Bellevue Avenue. c. 1908. The building to the far right is the edge of the King Block. Built between 1892-1893. Architect Perkins and Betton. Developed by LeRoy King and Gordon King.

Bellevue Avenue, Adrian [sic] Building and the Casino, Newport, R.I. c. 1919. The Audrain Building was designed by architect Bruce Price and built between 1902-1903. Built on part of the site of the old Atlantic House Hotel (which burned in 1898) by art dealer A.L. Audrain, it was noted for a glazed terra-cotta façade. The original shops included Audrains' art shop plus a stockbroker (Harriman & Co.) and clothing store. (Note the Brooks Brothers awning on the side of the building.) Standing and in use today.

Casino Court and Clock Tower, Newport, R.I. c. 1910. A view inside the Casino.

The Newport Casino, showing the Crescent Promenade, part of Tennis Courts and Squash Clubhouse, Newport, R.I. c.1910.

The Newport Casino, The Crescent, View from Entrance, Newport, R.I. c. 1908.

Court of the Casino, Newport, R.I. c. 1905.

Coaching Party at The Casino, Newport, R.I. c. 1905.

Tennis, Newport, R.I. c. 1925.

The Newport Horse Show, Four-in-hands before the Judges, Newport, R.I. c. 1911. The written message reads: "Dear Sister, Just a line let you know I'm getting along very good, isn't it too bad I won't need that little box this time. You can keep them till some other time. I will know better then. Love from us both Sadie."

Bellevue Avenue, Newport, R.I. c. 1910. This view is looking down Bellevue Avenue away from the Travers Block. The building on the left is the middle of Memorial Boulevard today.

Old Stone Mill, Newport, R.I. c.1910. Continuing up Bellevue, you come to Touro Park and the Stone Mill.

Touro Park, Statue of Commodore M.C. Perry, Newport, R.I. c. 1906. A view from Bellevue of Touro Park. The bandstand seen behind the statue of Perry is no longer standing.

Newport, R.I. The Redwood Library, said to be the oldest Public Library in America. c. 1920.

Hill Top Inn, Newport, R.I. c. 1919.

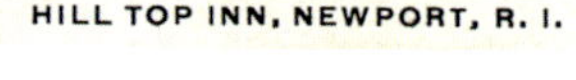

Hill-Top-Inn, Newport, Rhode Island. c. 1919. Original Newport home of William Morris Hunt, who sold the home in 1864 to his brother Richard Morris Hunt. Today, it is the site of The Viking Hotel at One Bellevue Avenue.

Chapter Four

Newport Beaches

There are nine beaches in Newport—some private, most public. In this chapter, we will show turn-of-the-century postcards with Newport beach scenes, both public and private. People in the late nineteenth and early twentieth centuries took the beach very seriously, viewing it as a form of entertainment. Newport's beaches were no exception. Easton's Beach or First Beach was a remarkable affair, featuring bathhouses, a roller coaster, restaurants, and a merry-go-round—all designed to make a day at the beach an event to be remembered. Among the private beaches, Bailey's Beach was a place to be seen by Newport's summer colony. Very private, very exclusive, and expensive by local standards, it was and still is a playground for the rich and famous.

Entrance to Newport Beach, Newport, R.I. c. 1932. Also called First Beach and Easton's Beach. Destroyed in the 1938 hurricane.

Bathing Casino, Newport Beach, Newport, R.I. In writing on the front of the card: *The open window is the dance hall where we play.* c. 1922. Destroyed in the 1938 hurricane.

Easton's Beach, Newport, R.I. c. 1907. The only thing that is the same today is the shoreline.

Roller Coaster, Newport Beach, R.I. c. 1918. Demolished.

Boardwalk Newport Beach, Newport, R.I. c. 1917. It can easily be seen from this postcard that Newport Beach was very popular.

Eastons Beach, Newport, R.I. c. 1912.

On the Beach at Newport, R.I. c. 1912.

Surf Bathing, Newport Beach, R.I. c. 1917.

Newport Beach, Showing The Cliff Walk, Newport, R.I. c. 1926. The mansion on the far left is The Breakers.

Along the Boardwalk, Newport Beach, R.I. c. 1915.

Newport, R.I. Bailey's Beach. View from the Cliff Walk. c. 1911. This is where the Cliff Walk ends.

Private Bathing House, Newport, R.I. c. 1922. Bailey's Beach.

Bath Houses of the "400," Newport, R.I. c. 1910. Bailey's Beach. Most of Bailey's buildings were destroyed in the 1938 hurricane.

Newport, R.I. Bailey's Beach, where the 400 bathe. c. 1912.

Bailey's Beach, Newport, R.I. c. 1950s.

Bibliography

Amory, Cleveland. *The Last Resorts.* New York: Harper & Bros., 1952.

Downing, Antoinette F., and Vincent Scully. *The Architectural Heritage of Newport Rhode Island 1640-1915.* Cambridge Mass: Harvard University Press, 1952.

Hopf, John T. *Newport Then and Now.* Newport, Rhode Island: John T. Hopf, 1982.

Elliott, Maude Howe. *This Was My Newport.* Cambridge: Mythology Co., 1944.

Edward, James G. *The Newport Story*. Newport, Rhode Island: Remington Ward, 1952.

Grayhurst, J.W. *Newport Casino Official Program 1904.* New York City: J.W. Grayhurst Publisher, 1904.

Jordy, William H. *Buildings of Rhode Island.* New York, New York: Oxford University Press, 2004.

Lehr, Elizabeth Drexel. *King Lehr and the Gilded Age.* Philadelphia: J.B. Lippincott Company, 1935.

Marquis, Albert Nelson. *Who's Who in New England.* Chicago: A.N. Marquis & Company, 1909.

Mason, George C. *Newport Illustrated.* Newport, Rhode Island: C.E. Hammett Jr. Publisher, 1854.

Morse, Jarvis M. *Rhode Island: A Guide to the Smallest State.* Boston: Houghton Mifflin Company, 1937.

Parmenter, Joseph G. *Newport: Capitol of Vacationland.* Newport, Rhode Island: Newport Chamber of Commerce, 1926.

Randall, Anne, and Robert P. Foley. *Newport: A Tour Guide*. Old Saybrook, Connecticut: Peregrine Press, 1983.

Sirkis, Nancy. *Newport Pleasures and Palaces.* New York: The Viking Press, 1963.

Stetson, Ruth M. *Newport Bulletin.* New York City: J.W. Grayhurst Publisher, 1930.

Washburn, Delphine. *Newport Tours of Estates Ocean Drive and Cliff Walk.* Fall River, Mass: Ellison Printing Co., Inc., 1963.

Yarnall, James L. *Newport Through Its Architecture: A History of Styles from Postmedieval to Postmodern.* Newport, Rhode Island: Salve Regina University Press, 2005.